Backyai
Birds

A HARPERCOLLINS NATURE STUDY BOOK

Backyard BIRDS

by Jonathan Pine
illustrated by Julie Zickefoose

HarperTrophy
A Division of HarperCollins*Publishers*

The illustrations in this book
were painted in watercolor and gouache on Strathmore paper.
Most of the birds were sketched from life.

Library of Congress Cataloging-in-Publication Data
Pine, Jonathan.
    Backyard birds / by Jonathan Pine ; illustrated by Julie Zickefoose.
       p.   cm.
    "A HarperCollins Nature Study Book."
    Summary: Provides information on the habits and behavior of house sparrows, starlings,
robins, wrens, hummingbirds, and nighthawks, with clues for easy identification.
    ISBN 0-06-021039-7. — ISBN 0-06-021040-0 (lib. bdg.)
    ISBN 0-06-446150-5 (pbk.)
    1. Birds—Juvenile literature.   2. Bird watching—Juvenile literature.   [1. Birds.
2. Bird watching.]   I. Zickefoose, Julie, ill.   II. Title.   III. Series.
QL676.2.M35   1993   91-45184
598—dc20   CIP
                                                                                   AC

First Harper Trophy edition, 1993.

The text of this book is for Mom,
whose Oklahoma backyard is a paradise for birds
—J. P.

To Ida and Dale
—J. Z.

Contents

Birds and Their Stories

This book is about six birds that live near people all across America. It tells just a little of each bird's story. The rest tells itself to anyone who watches to find out how these birds live near them.

A feeder and birdbath bring lots of birds close to a window. Binoculars make the smallest, shyest bird easy to see.

The best bird-watching outdoors begins with getting comfortable. At our house, we like to sit in the porch swing or on a garden bench. Sometimes we spread a blanket on the grass. Birds soon relax

around a relaxing human. It's all right to whisper, turn pages of a book, or raise binoculars slowly. Birds are frightened by sudden noise and motion.

We never get tired of watching the everyday adventures of our birds. They hunt food, drink and bathe, and fight to show who's boss. They sing, scold the cat, and vanish when they spy a hawk. They build secret nests. Many nests we see, but at a respectful distance. Others we never discover. But eggs do hatch and young do fly, some to live and some to die. It's a never-ending story.

Quick Little Birds and Bread

House sparrows live with people all around the world. On farms and in villages, in towns and great big cities, flocks of them hop and cheep, snatching up scraps and making quick escapes.

Dirty streets and greasy scraps do spoil their feathers in cities. Some people are surprised to see how pretty they are in cleaner, greener places.

House sparrows are really a kind of weaverbird from the dry plains of Africa. That must be why they love a nice hot dust bath. They flutter and fluff in it just as they do in water. Wet or dry, they clean and comb their feathers many times a day. All birds do.

A stout seed-cracking bill shows why house sparrows flock to bird feeders and fields of grain. They eat millions of weed seeds too.

House sparrows lead a busy, chattering life in flocks. All those pairs of sharp black eyes help spot food and danger. Even courtship draws a crowd. A male begins his dapper little dance, circling a female, hopping and cheeping. If she flies, he follows. Then others chase them till they all collide in a squabbling, tumbling free-for-all.

Each pair builds a messy nest of dry grass, paper, and light litter, especially feathers. The nest fills any kind of hole or is jammed in a tangle of vines or twigs. A neat inside pocket cradles five eggs. They are greenish blue speckled with gray and brown.

Many birds eat scraps of human food, but only house sparrows feed any directly to their young. They give babies bits of bread when insects can't be found. That's why they can nest downtown in big cities. Feeding bread helps house sparrows raise extra broods in early spring and fall, when cool weather reduces the supply of insects.

House sparrows know how to catch bugs around a house and yard. They fly up at walls to snatch resting beetles. First thing at sunup, they check porch lights

for moths. They hop down garden rows, inspecting lettuce leaves, studying each cabbage head. They are expert pickers of pesky hard-to-see green worms like the cabbage white butterfly caterpillar.

Even in a city street, busy with people and people's feet, these quick little birds find food to take away home. More of us should stop to watch which way they fly—with that bit of pizza pie!

Fine
Winter Feathers

If starlings were people, they'd be told to be more polite. At winter bird feeders they push and shove and grab and peck with that wickedly long sharp bill.

Sometimes it helps to offer starlings table scraps away from seed feeders. They like scraps better anyway. We give them just what they can gobble up quickly. Then they don't hang around all day.

After starlings eat, they wipe their bills clean before using them to comb their feathers smooth. This combing is called preening. All birds preen with oil from a special gland above the tail. You see birds reaching back to this gland. The oil helps

shape and waterproof the stiff feathers of back and wings and tail.

Starlings really are splendid winter birds. Their gleaming greenish purple feathers are dotted white like flakes of snow. In spring, their dark winter beaks turn a handsome yellow.

Most birds shed old feathers and grow new ones every year. This is called molting. Some birds molt twice a year. Starlings do. Their duller, blackish look in summer attracts less attention as they fly to and from the nest.

Starlings nest in all kinds of holes. Inside, a tangle of leaves and litter holds four to six eggs. They can be greenish white, white, or a lovely pale blue. When the eggs hatch, the babies soon grow loud and bold. We often hear the racket they make when food arrives.

Starlings are curious and clever eaters. They feed on seeds, fruit, berries, and some flying insects. Their specialty is hidden, crawling prey. They flip through

fallen leaves with that sharp spiked bill, nabbing bugs and worms.

Starlings move with a funny, tough-guy swagger because their legs are set far apart. This braces them for tug-of-war with beetle grubs in lawns. The legs help as the bird jabs down, grabs a fat grub, and wrestles it up through roots.

A starling's song is a long, rambling mixture of musical chirps, whistles, and

raspy wrong-sounding notes. It also mimics songs and calls of other birds. It's like someone switching from station to station on bird radio.

Most people find starlings hard to love. They do have some noisy, ruffian ways. But study them awhile. Listen to their crazy-quilt songs. Watch the sunlight stroke those beautiful winter feathers. Then make up your own mind.

A Bowl of Mud and Grass

We know spring is here when robins appear to sing *Cheer up! Cheer cheer cheer up!* The males come first, looking windblown, wild and wary. When females arrive, males start to fight. They fly up, pecking breast to breast. They lock beaks, wrestling on the ground. They may even fight themselves in shiny surfaces!

Male birds sing and fight to claim a space to feed and nest with a mate. Songs and threats save lots of fighting too.

Most robins build in trees, some high, some low. A few choose a funny location out in plain sight—a porch post, a fire escape, a mophead hanging on a wall! Even so, all birds fret about the safety of a nest. That's why we use binoculars to watch from a distance.

Robins work together. He brings dry grass and mud. She mixes them to make a stout bowl shape. By turning around and around inside, she makes it just her size. At last she lines it with fine dry grass.

Then she lays four famously lovely eggs. People call anything their color "robin's-egg blue." You may find bits of

shell dropped far from the nest, to hide the fact that eggs have hatched.

Most baby birds grow amazingly fast. Robins go from naked and helpless to feathered and flying in about two weeks. Even then, they must outgrow the spotted breast and soft wide bill of a nestling.

Sometimes one flies too soon. The old birds cry out in alarm as their baby flutters around, confused. We make sure no

cat is around, but otherwise don't try to help. Baby birds must learn to be wary of people as well as cats!

Young robins follow their parents across the lawn, learning how robins find food. The old birds cock their heads to look with one eye, then the other, for signs of a burrowing worm. Spotting one, they grab and pull! Baby runs up to beg, and is fed.

But young ones have to learn how to feed themselves. At first they look puzzled,

pecking at the grass. Then they catch on, and find worm after worm after worm.

Robins spend much of the day running and stopping, tilting their heads to study the ground. They catch all kinds of insects and crawling critters there. They also eat lots of berries and fruits.

Robins raise two or three broods a year, so there are plenty of robin families to watch all summer long. Then they fly south in autumn. The bare trees show us their empty nests filling with falling leaves.

A Tiny House for a Tiny Bird

This garden has a little pool, with flowers all around. There are daffodils and coral bells, sweet cicely, wild phlox and columbine, with pinks, lamb's ears, and bleeding heart. Ferns nestle against a mossy stump. In a little redbud tree is the smallest possible birdhouse.

The house wren has come to claim that house and all of the garden, too. These tiny birds are as bold and busy and bossy as any bird can be. It's hard to imagine a summer garden without its lively wrens.

The male arrives on a warm spring day. We hear him before we see him. His rising-and-falling, bubbling melody seems to say *Tsee-tsee-tsee-tsee Oodle-oodle-oodle.* It's a warning and a dare to other male house wrens. *"This place is mine!"* it says. *"Keep out or fight!"*

To females it says: *"Come be my mate and pick a nest."* He builds several in a hurry, in one hole after another. He stops only to eat and sing and sometimes fight. We see him tossing out old twigs and tucking new ones in. His energy is astonishing. He flies full speed to a small nest hole, popping in nonstop.

When a mate arrives, he goes a little crazy, singing and dancing, fluttering his wings. She follows him from nest to nest, each inside a cavity of some kind. One hole is in a tree, another in a toolshed wall. Others could be in crazy places. A wren will nest in an old shoe on a shelf, in a watering can or flowerpot, even in the pocket of a coat left hanging on a nail.

House wrens also use the homes we build for them. And we're in luck again this year. The female picks the birdhouse in the redbud right outside our kitchen window.

Her mate helps rearrange the twigs he put together so hastily. Then she lines the nest herself. Her six to eight brown speckled eggs will rest cozily in feathers, spider silk, and willow catkin down.

The female broods the eggs by herself,

but when they hatch, the male helps feed the chicks. After they fly, he may shepherd them around while she prepares to raise another brood.

Wrens live on insects and other hiding and crawling small life. Their hunt for food looks like hide-and-seek played in a garden and woodpile, in toolshed and garage. No wonder wrens think they own it all. They have explored every inch of the place!

Like Magic in the Air

Imagine a bird so small it can bathe in the dew on a rose. This bird weighs not much more than a penny, yet it can fly across the Gulf of Mexico. Its wings move so fast, they whir and blur. It can hover in one place in the air or dart forward and backward, up and down, and something like sideways too. Its feathers change color in the light. Its nest is made of spider silk. Flowers give it food.

Hundreds of kinds of amazing hummingbirds live in Central and South America. Only a few kinds live in the United States. Most are in the west, where there are rufous and black-chinned

hummers. East of the Rockies, the ruby-throated hummingbird follows the opening flowers north each spring. This is the bird we watch in our Oklahoma garden.

The male appeared one afternoon this April. He perched on a twig of the sweet-gum tree. Last year's hummingbird feeder had hung right there. We rushed to put it out again. We used the sugarwater mix recommended on the feeder box. More sugar would not be good. Oddly enough, hummingbirds would slowly starve on artificial sweeteners.

Hummingbirds eat more for their size than eagles or ostriches! Their flight burns that many calories. Hummers are quick and nimble, fierce little fighters. One will drive others away from feeders and flowers, zooming and swooping at incredible speeds, squeaking furiously.

Hummingbirds have their favorites,

like honeysuckle, but they sample flowers of many kinds and colors. We watch them zip from zinnia to zinnia on hot summer days. These dry, papery blooms come in every color, even lime green. The hummers bully the butterflies sipping zinnia nectar. They also find and eat tiny insects and spiders hiding in the petals.

The male's sideways, rocking court-ship flight is the only breeding behavior we can see. The female does all the work, but not where we are likely to see it.

Using spiderweb and bits of plants, she builds a tiny cup that sits on a twig. It can be five feet up, or fifty, and out over water too.

We've seen one nest in thirty years! It was right by a busy sidewalk, at eye level, almost invisible. But there it was, a tiny cup with two white eggs the size of little peas.

Still, even if you don't see hummingbird nests, one thing is certain. Young hummingbirds will appear as if by magic, and will fly like magic too.

High in the Sky

The nighthawk is not a hawk at all. Hawks have sharp beaks and claws like knives. The nighthawk's feet are weak and harmless. Her soft beak opens wide to catch insects as she flies. She is named for her swooping, hawklike flight.

The nighthawk is a sky bird. She is most often seen flying on wonderful, long, slim wings. Under each one is a broad, white band. You see it clearly as she climbs and swoops high up in the evening sky.

Swallows and swifts and martins also share the sky. But the nighthawk is easy to identify. She's larger and longer. Her wings flash white. Her mate's cry is a raspy *Peeent! Peeent! Peeent!*

The male nighthawk doesn't sing to attract a mate or challenge other males. He does something odd instead. He climbs sky-high, then dives headfirst. Down, down, down he speeds, then pulls up in a sudden graceful swoop. His stiff wing feathers brush the air just then with a loud, booming sound.

In May, the male nighthawk's display means that the female will soon be laying two eggs on the ground. The eggs sit out in the open, without any nest! Nighthawk, eggs, and chicks are all camouflaged with handsome speckles. Sitting still, they blend right in with stones and gravel.

Sometimes nighthawks nest right alongside busy roads. Others find safer stretches of gravel on the edges of parking lots.

The safest nighthawk nests may be in big cities. There, flat gravel roofs lift them high above traffic and enemies.

Nighthawks catch amazing numbers of

insects. One scientist found that a bird had eaten 500 mosquitoes in one flight. Another had 2,000 flying ants in its stomach.

Nighthawks bring their chicks pellets of crunched-up insects—bugs are real fast food. Nighthawks hatch out, grow up, and fly in just three weeks. Tricks they must learn include flying low over water to drink on the wing.

In August, large flocks of nighthawks

may gather above your town. There they drift slowly, lazily back and forth for several days before heading south. Their dozens and hundreds of white wing bars flash beautifully in the evening light.

After dark, we listen for their cries fading as they leave. Then it's nice to fall asleep and dream about nighthawks flying all winter long—above the green rain forests of South America.

Clues to These Six Backyard Birds

House Sparrow • Grown-up males have bold black bibs and chestnut markings. Females and young are duller gray and brown.

Starling • In winter, greenish purple feathers are dotted white. Feathers are duller in summer, without the white spots. Beak turns from black to yellow in spring.

Robin • Grayish brown with tawny orange breast. Female somewhat duller colored. Fledglings have spotted breast.

House Wren • Tiny bird with gray-brown feathers. Stubby tail held cocked up over its back.

Hummingbird • Tiniest of birds. Feathers glisten, changing colors in the sun. Brighter males show colorful throat patch.

Nighthawk • Mottled gray, brown, and white. Hard to see resting on the ground. In the sky, long pointed wings show bold white bars underneath. Male has white throat patch and band on tail.

Naming Birds We See

More than 800 kinds of birds live in the United States. Many are found in one area but not in others. This is why bird-watchers use books called guides to help identify the new birds they see. Bird-watching guides usually come in series, dividing the country into regions. Here are several series that can be found in bookstores and libraries everywhere:

The little *Golden Guides* (Racine, Wisconsin: Golden Press) are simple, inexpensive, and easy to use. They show the most common birds.

A more complete series is the famous one by Roger Tory Peterson (Boston: Houghton Mifflin Company).

The National Audubon Society issues a series that uses photographs (New York: Alfred A. Knopf, Inc.).

Every yard and neighborhood can be made a more attractive habitat for birds. Look for books such as:

Audubon Society Guide to Attracting Birds by Stephen W. Kress. (New York: Charles Scribner's Sons, 1985).